Pixie and the Bees

Words by Erica Richmond
Illustrations by Brooklin Holbrough

Copyright © 2020 by Open Sky Stories

All rights reserved. This book or any portion thereof
may not be reproduced or used in any manner whatsoever
without the express written permission of the publisher
except for the use of brief quotations in a book review.
First Printing, 2020
ISBN 978-1-7773505-0-5

Open Sky Stories
Peterborough, ON Canada
openskystories@gmail.com

www.openskystories.com

for everyone who has felt the bees fill their entire body with buzzing, I see you.

with deepest gratitude to my entire support team, professional and personal. Thank you for believing me.

Once upon a time in the not so distant past, there lived a Pixie. She loved to play. She loved to laugh. She was happy.

One day while she was out picking wild flowers in a field, Pixie came across a swarm of angry bees.

"What's the matter?" she asked. "Why are you so angry?"

They turned and looked at her with narrowed eyes. They were buzzing so loudly, the ground shook beneath them.

Pixie opened her mouth wide to scream, but before she could utter a sound, they all flew into her mouth and filled her entire body with buzzing.

She gasped and fell backwards.

She tried to spit them out, but they were too far down inside of her. She jumped up and down and tried to shake them out, but they hung on tight. She tried to plead them out but they refused to leave.

Not knowing what else to do, Pixie flew home while the bees filled her body with buzzing.

When she saw her friends, she tried to explain what had happened, but no one could believe her. This had never happened to them before, and they couldn't understand what she was talking about.

Pixie stood as close to them as possible.

"But this buzzing – can't you hear it?"

They shook their heads.

Pixie placed their hands on her chest.

"But this buzzing – can't you feel it?"

They shook their heads.

Pixie went to her doctor. He looked in her mouth and saw nothing. He looked in her ears and saw nothing. He listened to her chest but could not hear the buzzing. He inspected her wings, checked her dust supply and measured the points of her ears.

"There is nothing wrong with you," he said.

Embarrassed and confused and uncomfortable, Pixie went home. And she stayed there for a very long time, while the bees filled her body with buzzing.

They buzzed in her ears, making it hard to listen to anything else.

They buzzed in her chest, making it tight and hard to breathe.

They buzzed up and down her arms, making her squirm in discomfort.

They buzzed all night long.

Pixie was exhausted.

She tried to coax them out with honey, but they refused to leave.

She tried to scream them out, but the bees just buzzed louder.

She tried to cry them out, but not even her tears could wash them away.

She tried to ignore them, but they stung her and made her body ache.

Everything felt harder.

It was too hard for her to be with her friends. They couldn't understand what was wrong with her and why she was always screaming and crying and tired.

It was too hard for her to focus on anything else. She didn't want to play. She didn't want to laugh. Pixie was very unhappy.

So, she stayed home for a very long time, while the bees filled her body with buzzing.

One day Pixie mustered up enough energy to go for a bike ride. Very slowly she biked down the path and very slowly she breathed in the fresh air.

After some time, Pixie noticed that the bees had quieted, ever so slightly.

She kept biking.

They quieted even more.

She kept biking.

They barely made a sound.

Pixie let out a happy sigh and a bee flew out in her breath.

"Gasp!"

Pixie biked home, grinning and laughing and one bee lighter.

That night she lay in bed and as with every night, the bees filled her body with buzzing; though tonight there was one less bee.

Nervously, she took a deep breath in and slowly sighed.

Nothing happened.

She shifted in her bed.

Cautiously, she took another deep breath in and slowly sighed.

A single bee flew out.

Relieved, she took another deep breath in and slowly sighed.

Two bees flew out.

She did it again and again and again, taking deeper and deeper and deeper breaths until a few more bees flew out and the rest had quieted enough for her to fall sound asleep.

For the next few weeks, she kept biking and breathing, and more bees flew out in her breath. Things were better, but there were still many bees left inside her that filled her entire body with buzzing.

Pixie went back to her doctor.

"Watch." she said.

Pixie took a deep breath in and as she slowly exhaled a bee flew out in her breath.

"It's true!" he gasped.

Pixie cried with relief. More bees flew out.

The doctor made her a concoction of herbs and Pixie started taking it every day. This helped to quiet the bees, mostly.

Pixie kept biking and breathing every day and this helped to release the bees, mostly.

Things were never quite the same as they were before that day in the field. The bees never completely disappeared. Some days the bees still filled her body with buzzing. And some days Pixie still felt tired and uncomfortable and sick.

But she started to play again.

She started to laugh again.

And mostly, Pixie was happy.

Erica is the founder of Open Sky Stories and believes that words have the power to connect people. She lives in Peterborough, Ontario with her two teens finding joy, adventures and stories in everyday life. Pixie and the Bees is based on real life events and there are more Pixie stories to come.

Follow Erica on social media

@ OpenSkyStories or at openskystories.com

www.ingramcontent.com/pod-product-compliance
Lightning Source LLC
Chambersburg PA
CBHW051121110526
44589CB00026B/3000